DO DOGS COUNT?

DO DOGS COUNT?

Marion Carlson

Haystack Creatives
8270 Woodland Center Blvd
Tampa, Florida 33614
www.haystackcreatives.com

ISBN: 978-1-953115-44-7 (sc)
ISBN: 978-1-953115-43-0 (e)

One to ten
Let's count—

0

0 and 0 are 0

Zero is no one, zip!

0 No one

1

is me, I am only one.

Here I am, all alone, sitting on a great big stone! Just one is not fun.

2

is me and you
1 and 1 are 2

What should we do?
I know, we'll go to the zoo!

3

is me, you, and she
2 and 1 are 3

The bird is third.
All three of us are looking at
monkeys swinging in a tree.

4

is me, you, she and 1 more.
3 and 1 are 4

We four are going out the door!

4 is the monkey 

5

is 4 and 1 more
4 and 1 are 5

Jumping rope for five – sakes alive!

5 is the butterfly 

6

is one and five tired from their rope tricks.
5 and 1 are 6

Five lying in a row when along comes Joe. He'll help us get up and go.

6 is Joe 

7

is 6 of us and here comes Kevin.
6 and 1 are 7

All seven of us sitting on a fence in suspense.

7 is Kevin 

8

is 7 of us and along comes Nate.
7 and 1 are 8

All eight wait on the gate. Soon someone will bring lots of food on a great big plate.

8 is Nate 

9

is 8 and one more is just fine.
8 and 1 are 9

Here we are, all nine hanging out on a line!

9 is the squirrel 

10

is the whole gang plus Gwen.
Here is Gwen, so now we are 10.
9 and 1 are 10

Now we can start all over again
or we can count some more --

--here we go!

0+0=0	10+0=10	0+0=0
1+0=1	10+1=11	10+0=10
1+1=2	10+2=12	10+10=20
1+2=3	10+3=13	10+20=30
1+3=4	10+4=14	10+30=40
1+4=5	10+5=15	10+40=50
1+5=6	10+6=16	10+50=60
1+6=7	10+7=17	10+60=70
1+7=8	10+8=18	10+70=80
1+8=9	10+9=19	10+80=90
1+9=10	10+10=20	10+90=100

All this counting is to show that our number system is base 10. Don't miss the rhyming words that are spelled differently.

Do dog's really count?

Maybe not numbers, but most of the time they count in many ways as a pet for you and me!

We're done, have fun!

CPSIA information can be obtained
at www.ICGtesting.com
Printed in the USA
BVHW051159060521
606650BV00014B/1805

9 781953 115447